MW00619058

HELLO
HOPE YOU ENJOY
THIS AND PASS IT ON
WHEN YOU'RE DONE.
— BRUNO.

i get the feeling

when this is over i'll still

avoid most people

Bruno Pieroni

i get the feeling

when this is over i'll still

avoid most people

two whole years at home
said i'd learn a new language
wrote haiku instead

Copyright ©2022 Bruno Pieroni

All rights reserved. No part of
this book may be reproduced
in any form or by any electronic
or mechanical means, including
information storage and
retrieval systems, without
permission in writing from the
publisher, except by reviewers,
who may quote brief passages
in a review.

text, cover and book design by
Bruno Pieroni

Printed and bound in the USA
First printing April 2022
www.brunopieroni.com

so, is this where the

table of contents should go?

asking for a friend

never a good sign

reading the words "last-minute

all-office meeting"

Mar 16, 2020, 4:07 PM

"we'll probably see

you in a couple of weeks"

did we jinx ourselves?

Mar 17, 2020, 11:12 PM

not to brag but yeah

my bank just told me we are

in this together

Mar 18, 2020, 8:55 PM

listen we survived

maroon 5; we'll make it through

this covid-19

so what base is it

when they let you quarantine

with them and their food

Mar 20, 2020, 9:27 AM

already getting

"i feel like i'm grounded" vibes

one week into this

Mar 21, 2020, 1:48 PM

once upon a time

"how are you holding up" texts

were reserved for sports

Mar 22, 2020, 7:19 AM

if i had bought stock

in the phrase "uncertain times"

i could afford meat

Mar 24, 2020, 3:24 PM

look i'll be ok

if i never hear the words

"wet market" again

Mar 25, 2020, 9:29 AM

who else agrees this

toilet paper shortage is

a big bidet ploy?

Mar 27, 2020, 1:23 PM

social distancing

or as we like to call it

introvert heaven

Mar 28, 2020, 4:17 PM

there's no place like home

there's no place like home because

nothing is open

Mar 30, 2020, 10:45 PM

hey celebrities

your "imagine" video

kinda made things worse

Mar 31, 2020, 4:33 PM

winnie the pooh and

donald the duck: patron saints

of shirt and no pants

birds, planes and sirens

where did city noises go?

the air sounds creepy

Apr 3, 2020, 7:33 PM

hulu on ipad

netflix on television

sometimes vice-versa

Apr 5, 2020, 2:52 PM

my milkshake brings all

the boys to the yard and i'm

like: six feet away!

Apr 6, 2020, 8:02 PM

krasinski, fauci,

jordan, and exotic too

lockdown's mount rushmore

Apr 7, 2020, 12:05 PM

are we ignoring

the elephant in the zoom?

(that joke's my king lear)

last time i saw a

coworker's bedroom this much

HR got involved

Apr 9, 2020, 7:20 AM

found myself asking

what day of the week is it?

as if it mattered

Apr 10, 2020, 10:08 PM

what if we could buy

(and i'm just spitballing here)

pre-washed groceries

when i wear a mask

i can't stop quoting "the mask"

sssssomebody stop me!

pro tip: pretend you're

eight years old and this virus

is called "cooties"

may your living room

be your office but also

your secret nap room

Apr 14, 2020, 8:57 AM

remember back when

we checked our weather app in

the morning? good times

Apr 16, 2020, 6:27 PM

not gonna lie, y'all

i feel bad for free hugs guy

what will he do now

everyone in masks

guess we're all gonna have to

get good at smizing

before quarantine:

on computer all day long

during: same but more

Apr 23, 2020, 7:01 PM

what is the point of

clapping for heroes and then

voting for villains

Apr 27, 2020, 2:19 PM

dance like there's no one

watching (but yo, cover your

webcam just in case)

Apr 30, 2020, 12:20 PM

took out the garbage

glad to find one excuse to

step outside today

May 3, 2020, 8:11 AM

day fifty: we've reached

the "you chew too loud" part of

this here quarantine

May 4, 2020, 1:32 PM

i run in place, stuff

my cheeks and do it again

am i part hamster?

whenever i miss

the office i buy one-ply

toilet paper. done.

half my exercise

nowadays is muting and

unmuting myself

in the morning i

stare out windows, later i

stare out more windows

May 8, 2020, 1:08 AM

sometimes i feel like

i'm the only one taking

this seriously

May 11, 2020, 4:29 PM

i've been going through

so much hand sanitizer

maybe don't eat it?

i'll start worrying

the day we begin missing

airplane middle seats

May 13, 2020, 5:41 PM

the murder hornets:

minor league baseball team or

ska band? you decide.

May 15, 2020, 7:45 PM

why'd no one tell me

the great british baking show

was soothing as fuck

May 17, 2020, 11:34 AM

TMI, i know:

just tested positive for

donation fatigue

every day, same time

we clap, clank pots, and go, "wait,

it's night already?"

May 19, 2020, 9:57 PM

been learning so much

like, "hydroxychloroquine:"

six syllables long!

May 20, 2020, 9:14 AM

no subways breaking

no bad traffic to deal with

i'm still late for work

May 21, 2020, 9:49 PM

i guess i gave up

going anywhere for lent

and then never stopped

May 23, 2020, 8:57 PM

these are fucked-up times

doctors wearing garbage bags

body-armored cops

May 24, 2020, 1:02 AM

bandana face masks:

now you can save grandma's life

and be a cowboy

May 25, 2020, 3:18 PM

this is the way the

world ends: not with a bang but

while we do puzzles

May 26, 2020, 7:21 PM

they made it through the

1918 flu without

grubhub; you can too

ok sing with me:

you scream, i scream, we all scream

when we watch the news

May 29, 2020, 8:23 PM

never thought being

part of history would be

this black mirror-y

May 30, 2020, 3:23 PM

props to those people

who found a way to get out

lucky astronauts

Jun 1, 2020, 7:50 PM

it's ironic that

i get curvier the more

i flatten the curve

Jun 2, 2020, 4:33 PM

congratulations

if you posted a black square

everything is fixed

Jun 3, 2020, 8:30 PM

if you're not angry

you're not paying attention

so we're in the streets

Jun 4, 2020, 9:32 PM

curfews are easy

when you have been practicing

staying home for months

Jun 5, 2020, 10:06 PM

is it just me or

doesn't the last month feel like a

bad movie montage

Jun 7, 2020, 9:43 PM

shit what if the light

at the end of the tunnel

is just a fire truck

Jun 8, 2020, 9:47 AM

every day: the same

and yet mondays still suck big,

hairy, donkey balls

Jun 9, 2020, 6:22 PM

because distancing

i take the road less traveled

call me robert frost

Jun 11, 2020, 11:29 AM

there's a difference

between being homesick and

sick of being home

Jun 12, 2020, 5:59 PM

if you miss statues

of racists, which one are you:

racist or pigeon?

i stretch every day

to parkour out of the way

of dudes without masks

Jun 14, 2020, 3:01 PM

have we tried sending

kendall jenner out to hand

a cop a pepsi

Jun 16, 2020, 11:22 PM

"how am i doing?"

dude i just teared up thinking

of food truck tacos

i don't know who needs

to hear this but your mistress

wants to hear from you

Jun 20, 2020, 7:12 PM

a fun thing to do

is read a book and not get

into facebook fights

Jun 21, 2020, 7:40 AM

naked and afraid:

reality show or just

a good shower cry

Jun 22, 2020, 11:35 AM

have we considered

unplugging the country and

plugging it back in

"time is canceled" or

"i can't believe yesterday

was a week ago"

Jun 27, 2020, 2:52 PM

tiny living space

watched through webcams; am i a

zoo animal now?

Jun 28, 2020, 11:28 AM

all leap years are weird

but none ever leapt into

turd fires like this one

Jun 30, 2020, 5:10 PM

slap me if i ask

"does mcdonald's deliver?"

ba da ba ba ba

Jul 2, 2020, 8:33 PM

we didn't start the fire

it was always burning since

in the before times

walking outside is

saying "remember that place?"

over and over

Jul 5, 2020, 6:15 PM

wear your mask over

(and i can't stress this enough)

both your mouth and nose

Jul 6, 2020, 2:55 AM

can't sleep; brain buzzing

when will the vaccine come out

how does a belt work

moving towns right now

feels like an irish goodbye

and it breaks my heart

Jul 11, 2020, 10:27 AM

air pollution: down

toilet paper: back on shelves

nature is healing

Jul 12, 2020, 9:04 AM

camera off and

microphone off that's the way

we like our meetings

wish number one: peace

wish number two: a vaccine

last wish: a haircut

Jul 16, 2020, 5:57 PM

just realized that

quarantine rhymes with vaccine

bad sign for music

Jul 18, 2020, 12:33 AM

my nightly mantra:

this has been the worst news day

well, since yesterday

Jul 20, 2020, 4:53 PM

nice try, summer day

but this is "the new normal"

we work nine to nine

Jul 22, 2020, 3:29 PM

when i miss starbucks

i burn my own coffee and

shout my own name wrong

Jul 24, 2020, 8:56 AM

surprised i still haven't

seen anyone walking 'round

in full scuba gear

cardboard fans in stands

are creepy. thanks for coming

to my masterclass

Jul 27, 2020, 8:04 AM

happy wednesday, y'all!

hold on, it's thursday, though, right?

nope it's still monday

Jul 28, 2020, 7:51 AM

stages of lockdown:

gonna read books; netflix; bread;

scream into pillows

Jul 30, 2020, 10:32 PM

how do we keep a

life outside of work when there's

no outside of work

Jul 31, 2020, 3:02 PM

"oh god, i sure hope

my microphone was just off"

spoiler: it was not

Aug 1, 2020, 1:23 PM

i remember when

we called it the "great outdoors"

now it's "wait indoors"

Aug 3, 2020, 3:36 PM

wait up: baby boom?

who's looking around going

"great time to not sleep"

what i lack in pants

i make up for in saving

money on laundry

Aug 6, 2020, 12:46 PM

one drive-thru window

and one benihana chef

that's my shark tank pitch

Aug 8, 2020, 12:27 AM

is today the day

i lose it, download tiktok

and lip sync to "jump"

Aug 10, 2020, 4:22 PM

apologies friends

who i made spend months learning

our complex handshakes

Aug 13, 2020, 7:52 PM

keep your friends close and

your enemies closer sounds

like bad advice now

Aug 14, 2020, 1:30 PM

maybe not today,

maybe not this week, but soon

gonna weigh myself

Aug 16, 2020, 10:36 PM

please remember to

save the country by *checks notes*

...buying tons of stamps?

Aug 17, 2020, 8:26 AM

a new week begins

i'm either working from home

or homing from work

i own enough books

to make myself feel happy

and movers angry

i'm a normal guy

i put every face mask on

one ear at a time

Aug 23, 2020, 11:29 PM

guess it's an honor

but i'm still thrown by the words

"you're in our pod now"

Aug 24, 2020, 6:56 PM

i know the name of

the postmaster general

and i don't want to

Aug 27, 2020, 2:01 PM

i say "i miss ya"

a lot for someone who is

loving staying in

Aug 29, 2020, 1:58 PM

week days i stare at

myself on zoom calls, weekends

i stare at my phone

hey twenty-twenty,

none of any of this was

on my vision board

it's hard to believe

i have been stuck inside for

twelve pounds already

"no, go ahead, please

you break this instead of me:"

why we hire movers

Sep 7, 2020, 3:41 PM

which is scarier:

a "we need to talk" text or

clicking "share my screen"

i wish i could say

"can everyone mute themselves"

outside of zoom too

Sep 11, 2020, 12:04 AM

all i'm saying is

i miss those simpler days when

the floor was lava

Sep 15, 2020, 9:08 AM

oh shit the first time

someone sneezes on the train

gonna be mayhem

Sep 19, 2020, 7:59 PM

next lockdown pro tip:

bring a loved one and/or a

cast iron skillet

Sep 21, 2020, 5:40 PM

among many things

this virus finally killed

the five second rule

an eighties haiku:

up, up, down, down, left, right, left,

right, B, A and start

Sep 25, 2020, 7:06 PM

losing it today

thought i'd try to tie a tie

failed miserably

Sep 27, 2020, 4:27 PM

sad movie or not

when theaters reopen

there'll be much crying

Sep 29, 2020, 9:47 PM

did this cheetoface

just say "stand back and stand by?"

not a bad sign, right?

5pm we switch

from our work browser tabs to

our fun browser tabs

Oct 2, 2020, 6:54 PM

"hey i'm walking here!"

sorry, trying to blend in

with these new yorkers

we're all tired. no one

even hopes this email finds

me well anymore

Oct 7, 2020, 5:04 PM

a strong gust of wind

we all run after our masks

holding our breaths in

Oct 10, 2020, 7:05 PM

irony: thanks to

an invisible virus

i can't see my friends

once there's a vaccine

i might spend the next six months

at karaoke

Oct 13, 2020, 10:04 AM

don't stop believin'

hold on to that feelin' yeah

streetlight, people-oooooh

and then one day all

seven p.m. applause died

we were still working

Oct 20, 2020, 8:11 PM

what do we want? desks

when do we want it? next week

fine, in six months then

Oct 21, 2020, 7:22 AM

do my workmates know

how many presentations

i've designed from bed?

Oct 23, 2020, 12:24 AM

debate drinking game:

drink every time... no, fuck it

drink the entire time

Oct 25, 2020, 7:36 PM

work from home day one:

shower before zoom meeting

month seven: during

Oct 29, 2020, 5:02 PM

"shit-faced or plastered?"

i get those mixed up after

just one wine glass now

Nov 1, 2020, 6:08 PM

this new citizen

just voted for the first time

will it be worth it

Nov 3, 2020, 1:32 AM

u.s. elections

we know who'll get the most votes

but not who will win

Nov 6, 2020, 2:15 PM

if your election

is lasting over four days

then call your doctor

Nov 7, 2020, 11:48 AM

CNN: "biden"

now brooklyn sounds like brazil

when we win world cups

Nov 8, 2020, 12:23 PM

looks like the host of

celebrity apprentice

lost his job again

Nov 9, 2020, 5:21 PM

dark at five again

what difference does it make

still nowhere to go

Nov 12, 2020, 9:14 AM

if it will be a

"camera on" type meeting

tell me in advance

Nov 13, 2020, 10:10 AM

"do you have covid?

because man you have no taste"

— me at rap battles

i have ranked all my

coworkers in order of

clearest microphone

go shawty, it's your

birthday we gon' party like

it's a zoom again

there's nothing wrong with

staying home to read haiku

while the world crumbles

Nov 19, 2020, 10:03 PM

give it to me straight

how long do i have to live

(sneezed into my mask)

Nov 22, 2020, 8:15 AM

we missed a good chance

to start walking around in

giant hamster balls

Nov 25, 2020, 9:52 PM

bad day for soccer

too little maradona

too much VAR

Nov 28, 2020, 8:47 PM

if you don't find food

when you open the fridge just

open it again

Dec 1, 2020, 9:25 PM

riding a packed train

to email a coworker?

no way, offices

Dec 3, 2020, 12:38 PM

i just want to be

able to look back and say

"showered every day"

Dec 7, 2020, 12:20 PM

who are these people

who are still matching their socks

day in and day out?

Dec 10, 2020, 3:10 PM

look on the bright side

we're all safe from that guy who

wears too much cologne

Dec 17, 2020, 9:34 PM

kids are cool but man

glad i'm not homeschooling

anyone right now

Dec 20, 2020, 8:59 PM

i cannot believe

another week has gone by

not watching "the wire"

Dec 23, 2020, 12:10 AM

just one day without

one beep from microsoft teams

my full christmas list

Dec 31, 2020, 9:27 AM

i'm glad years are not

like soccer because we'd have

months of stoppage time

Jan 5, 2021, 9:59 PM

thanks to this year we

now know the name of every

county in georgia

Jan 6, 2021, 4:52 PM

january sixth

like a fyre festival for

stupid coup attempts

five hate languages:

fascism, racism, bigotry,

sexism and fox news

Jan 13, 2021, 1:05 AM

wait up, sea shanties

are blowing up on tiktok?

go home, year, you're drunk

Jan 16, 2021, 3:10 PM

as kids we wished for

snow days so badly, now that's

all we friggin' have

was missing concerts

turned the music real loud

stomped on my own foot

Jan 23, 2021, 7:39 AM

you'll never convince

me that moviepass didn't see

all of this coming

Jan 27, 2021, 5:20 PM

and one week later

i am still photoshopping

mitten bernie memes

Feb 2, 2021, 10:11 AM

and on groundhog day

no shadow of a vaccine

six more months of zoom

Feb 7, 2021, 9:24 PM

congrats tom brady

but back home we still call you

gisele bündchen's hubs

when i said i missed

chicago i meant decent

tacos not blizzards

Feb 11, 2021, 7:50 AM

a blanket of snow

silencing sounds like it's a

mute button for life

Feb 15, 2021, 3:29 PM

if i'd known about

masks i for sure wouldn't have spent

thousands on braces

Feb 16, 2021, 11:57 PM

the vaccine is here!

but i'm two hundred million

and eighty in line

Feb 17, 2021, 6:11 PM

moderna? pfizer?

johnson and johnson? who cares

here's my arm, have fun

Feb 18, 2021, 7:55 PM

mars rover made it

to another planet. me?

not even the beach

Feb 21, 2021, 7:21 PM

just heard my grandpa

got his vaccine. which of you

is chopping onions?

Feb 25, 2021, 8:41 AM

scream inside your heart?

there's half a million dead; scream

outside of it too

Feb 27, 2021, 9:40 PM

i'm in a book club

but i'm the only member

fuck yeah there's still wine

Feb 28, 2021, 2:50 PM

who's ready to play:

is it just allergies or

is it the covid

Mar 1, 2021, 10:51 PM

crap crap crap crap crap

tested positive today

crap crap crap crap crap

Mar 2, 2021, 3:54 PM

hell hath no fury

like someone who never leaves

home learning he's sick

sick stages: grumpy,

dopey, happy, bashful, doc,

sneezy and sleepy

somebody once told

me the world's gonna roll me

is this what they meant

Mar 5, 2021, 9:45 AM

lost my sense of smell

before summer in new york

maybe good timing?

i feel stupid and

contagious here we are now,

home quarantining

Mar 7, 2021, 1:26 PM

feeling better; now

if i could have that sense of

smell back that'd be great

Mar 10, 2021, 5:07 PM

i still remember

every single travel plan

from this time last year

Mar 12, 2021, 4:32 PM

the expectation:

one year, one hundred books read

reality: nope

Mar 13, 2021, 11:01 PM

one year ago it

was friday the thirteenth; been

like that ever since

Mar 14, 2021, 9:58 AM

no way someone hates

daylight saving time change day

more than flavor flav

home is where you don't

have to minimize windows

unexpectedly

Mar 26, 2021, 8:13 AM

well, well, well, if it

isn't QR codes suddenly

making a comeback

tried to write haiku

about the suez canal

but that ship has sailed

please be respectful

some of us are doing this

with no dogs to pet

Mar 31, 2021, 1:39 PM

one day it happened

phone call, the word "aunt" followed

by "intubated"

Apr 2, 2021, 4:15 AM

they said "soon we'll all

know someone who died of this"

then it was my turn

Apr 9, 2021, 8:35 AM

no goodbyes allowed

no leaning on each other

a livestreamed mass

Apr 10, 2021, 12:23 PM

after this lockdown

let's celebrate half-birthdays

for the next few years

Apr 11, 2021, 12:58 PM

my vaccine sticker

is cool plus there's a bonus:

got the vaccine too

Apr 13, 2021, 7:15 AM

vaccine side effect

like an instagram story

gone in just a day

Apr 16, 2021, 6:20 PM

assembling new desk

shouted new curse words, missed the

office for first time

Apr 19, 2021, 1:38 PM

someday the question

"can everyone see my screen"

will take us way back

Apr 23, 2021, 9:24 AM

this quarantine is

like a box of chocolates

it makes me fatter

Apr 26, 2021, 11:50 AM

job interview in

ten minutes. quick, how do you

zoom a firm handshake?

May 1, 2021, 3:23 PM

people still wearing

the same pants since this began

what is your secret

May 4, 2021, 11:53 PM

"no one knows what's in them vaccines," morons say as they chew on hot dogs

May 7, 2021, 5:25 PM

"great resignation?"

well i just quit my job and

it did feel awesome

May 14, 2021, 4:11 PM

sunglasses and mask

or as i like to call it

the reverse batman

May 20, 2021, 3:35 PM

"my precious," i say

to the vaccination card

i'll show everywhere

May 26, 2021, 11:43 AM

here's an idea

take the time today to thank

your wifi router

Jun 1, 2021, 6:55 AM

remote job, first day

need to make good impression

ironed my sweatpants

Jun 7, 2021, 6:01 PM

"i'm vaccinated"

"i am vaccinated too"

feels better each time

Jun 15, 2021, 3:16 PM

dressy shirt on top

gym shorts below, a.k.a.

the zoom call mullet

Jun 22, 2021, 3:55 PM

what if this is how

we learn we should have always

been working barefoot

Jul 1, 2021, 8:52 AM

meeting coworkers

is everyone gonna be

taller in person

Jul 7, 2021, 4:15 PM

that which doesn't kill you

is going to mutate so

get vaccinated

Jul 16, 2021, 7:33 AM

coffeepot gurgles

my heart races me awake

pavlov would be proud

Jul 26, 2021, 8:58 AM

so many haikus

trust me yet or are you still

counting syllables?

Aug 7, 2021, 8:11 AM

maybe one day i'll

be as brave as those who bike

wearing their airpods

my tombstone will read

"never wished someone happy

birthday on linkedin"

Aug 23, 2021, 4:50 PM

won't somebody think

of all the horses walking

around full of worms?

Sep 1, 2021, 8:26 AM

ocean is on fire

and now there's a hurricane

apocalypse much?

Sep 4, 2021, 11:12 PM

climate change? nah just

once in a millennium

weather twice this year

Sep 7, 2021, 9:28 PM

don't take your mask off

in front of anyone else

this is the way y'all

Sep 12, 2021, 9:56 AM

don't hate the player

hate the open plan office

we'll still go back to

Sep 18, 2021, 3:47 PM

coming out of my

cage and i've been doing just

fine? nope still worried

Sep 24, 2021, 11:49 PM

i don't know about

you guys but i was promised

some roaring twenties

Oct 4, 2021, 9:38 AM

who am i to judge

but fingerless gloves are like

flip-flops for your hands

Oct 9, 2021, 1:03 PM

all the leaves are brown

and the sky is grey: one star

would not recommend

Oct 13, 2021, 7:18 AM

"be the no bones day

you want to see in the world"

— me being gen z

Oct 22, 2021, 1:02 AM

maybe the real

squid game was the burnout we

dodged along the way

Oct 26, 2021, 8:05 AM

"hot desking" sounds gross

and grosser when you learn what

it really means

Oct 31, 2021, 9:59 PM

if there's not at least

ten ted lassos it's not a

halloween party

Nov 7, 2021, 1:25 PM

staring at myself

all the way through this meeting

it's a good hair day

Nov 15, 2021, 6:09 PM

i miss forgetting

all the passion with which i

hate ticketmaster

Nov 20, 2021, 7:03 AM

i like my coffee

like i like my booster shot:

keeping me alive

forget the canned stuff

this thanksgiving make supply

chain issues from scratch

Nov 29, 2021, 9:12 AM

in a pandemic

every single monday is

already cyber

Dec 2, 2021, 8:59 PM

four great things, one vile

my spotify wrapped or this

whole year, really

Dec 10, 2021, 6:03 PM

for sure there must be

a german word for how far

these swab tests go in

Dec 16, 2021, 7:10 PM

new york reopened

overnight like a switch and

closed back the same way

i don't want a lot

for christmas, there's just one thing

i need: at home tests

Dec 31, 2021, 9:58 PM

twenty twenty two

twenty twenty one again

twenty twenty too

Jan 1, 2022, 9:12 AM

january 1st

same "not seen since last year" joke

this year it's more true

Jan 7, 2022, 9:58 PM

remember when we

didn't know about variants

those were some good times

dearly beloved

we've gathered here today to

share our wordle scores

Jan 26, 2022, 8:59 PM

worldwide pandemics

had previously looked much

better in movies

Feb 4, 2022, 11:43 AM

snow and rain and sleet

all that staying inside feels

underrated now

god made mugs so

that we could literally

give coffee a hug

Feb 13, 2022, 10:05 PM

super bowl over,

we return to a life of

skipping commercials

Feb 17, 2022, 8:11 PM

inside you there are

two wolves: neither of them can

explain NFTs

Feb 25, 2022, 7:13 PM

hey marie kondo

motions towards everything

this does not spark joy

Feb 28, 2022, 1:21 AM

lying in bed late

phone light shines on our faces

now and then we groan

Mar 4, 2022, 8:43 PM

something about this

"nuclear plant is on fire" thing

doesn't sit right with me

Mar 9, 2022, 6:35 PM

and long story short

let's not go back to normal

turns out normal sucked

Mar 13, 2022, 4:46 PM

two years into this,

no meetings that could have been

emails were emails

Mar 16, 2022, 5:48 PM

so, TL;DR

two years; wrote lots of haiku

didn't start a podcast

tomorrow morning

we return to the office

i search "small talk how"

Mar 28, 2022, 8:59 AM

at last: one train and

two elevators later

i click "join meeting"

—

masks on, we've gone out
because it was important
to say these names loud:

ahmad aubery
trayvon martin, botham jean
george floyd, freddie gray

breonna taylor
sandra bland, eric garner
philando castile

laquan mcdonald
michael brown, alton sterling
david mcatee

oscar grant, sean reed
walter scott, tony mcdade
and joão pedro

thanks casey, ally,

ben, kyle, peter, brad and you

yes, you reading this

about the author:

bruno pieroni would

love to see your pets

please check out and follow
@haikusfromlastnight

@HAIKUS FLN

to tia katia

Made in the USA
Middletown, DE
15 April 2022

64028421R00163